NORM AND AHMED

ALEX BUZO

CURRENCY PRESS
SYDNEY

CURRENCY PLAYS

First published in 1969 in *Komos*, Vol.2 No.2.

This edition first published in 2014
Currency Press Pty Ltd,
PO Box 2287, Strawberry Hills, NSW, 2012, Australia
enquiries@currency.com.au
www.currency.com.au

Cataloguing-in-publication data for this title is available from the National Library of Australia website: www.nla.gov.au

Front cover shows Craig Meneaud (left) as Ahmed, and Laurence Coy as Norm, in The Alex Buzo Company's 2007 production at The Old Fitzroy Hotel Theatre, Sydney. (Photo by Mark Mawson)

Contents

Currency Press acknowledges the Traditional Owners of the Country on which we live and work. We pay our respects to all Aboriginal and Torres Strait Islander Elders, past and present.

Norm and Ahmed was first performed by the Old Tote Theatre Company at the Old Tote Theatre, Sydney, on 9 April 1968, with the following cast:

NORM	Ron Graham
AHMED	Edwin Hodgeman

Director, Jim Sharman
Set Designer, Allan Lees

CHARACTERS

NORM, a strongly-built, middle-aged man

AHMED, a slim, young Pakistani student.

SETTING

A footpath on a Sydney street under some scaffolding in front of a construction site. A white fence at the back, about five feet high, and then a wire-mesh fence rising above it. The scaffolding is supported by two posts at the front, which are joined by a handrail. There is a bus stop on one side and a garbage bin on the other.

TIME

Midnight on a summer night.

Lights up on NORM, *who is leaning against the fence. He wears an open-necked white shirt and grey trousers. A clock strikes twelve.* NORM *moves around restlessly looking up and down the street. He takes out a cigarette packet, looks in it, then screws it up and flings it on the ground angrily. He brings out a fresh packet, rips off the cellophane with his teeth and takes out a cigarette, which he lights with a lighter. He moves around a bit more and then leans on the fence again. He waits. Then he starts moving around some more, and suddenly straightens up, looking to his left. He puts his cigarette out and takes another from the packet, putting it in his mouth unlit. He leans casually against the fence. The sound of footsteps is heard and* AHMED *appears, wearing a Nehru-style suit and carrying a briefcase. He walks past* NORM.

NORM: Excuse me, mate.

AHMED *stops and looks at* NORM. *Pause.*

Got a light?

AHMED: Yes, certainly.

He offers a box of matches.

NORM: Thanks.

He keeps the matches after he has lit up.

I was dying for a smoke. Lucky you turned up. Nothing open at this hour.

AHMED: No, it's nearly midnight.

Pause. AHMED *has been waiting for* NORM *to return his*

matches, but now he starts to edge away warily.

NORM: Wait a minute, mate.

AHMED: Yes?

Pause.

NORM: You forgot your matches.

He holds them out.

AHMED: [*taking them warily*] Thank you.

He edges away.

NORM: What's the matter, mate? Do you think going to hold you up and rob you or something?

AHMED: [*hastily*] Oh no, not at all.

NORM: This isn't India, mate. You're in Sydney. No Bombay stranglers around here. You're quite safe.

AHMED: There are hoodlums here, too. Just as many as in my country.

NORM: Yeah, I'd reckon it'd be about evens. What part of the… uh… south-east Asian sub-continent would you be from?

AHMED: I am from Pakistan. Karachi, to be exact. I, uh, really must be going…

NORM: Eh, wait a minute, mate. I'm not going to rob you or bash you or anything.

AHMED: I was not suggesting for one minute that you were.

NORM: Then what's the matter, you think I'm a drunk? You think I'm one of those old pisspots who go around the place annoying decent people?

AHMED: No, not at all.

NORM: You think I'm a poofter, then, don't you? That's what you're thinking, isn't it? You think I'm like those poofters in Hyde Park who go around soliciting blokes.

AHMED: Certainly not. I assure you I think nothing of the kind. I hope I have not insulted you in any way. If I have, I crave your forgiveness.

NORM: Ar, she's right. I suppose you've got to be careful these days. Lot of nasty types around.

AHMED: Yes, there is a lot of violence prevalent at the moment.

NORM: Too right. You look a bit uneasy.

AHMED: I do?

NORM: Yes. Are you sure you're all right?

AHMED: Yes.

NORM: You don't look all right.

AHMED: I feel fine.

NORM: My name's Norm Gallagher, what's yours?

AHMED: My name is Ahmed. [*Moving away*] Well, I don't wish to seem rude…

NORM: Pleased to meet you, Ahmed.

He offers his hand.

AHMED: [*shaking hands*] How do you do?

NORM: Pakistan. Now that's an interesting place. I've never been to Pakistan. I was in Egypt during the war, but we never went anywhere else. How do you like Australia?

AHMED: It is a very nice place. Naturally I tend to get a little homesick at times, but I quite like it out here. The people are very friendly.

NORM: It's good to hear that, Ahmed. You feel you're settling down all right?

AHMED: Yes, I think so. One always experiences difficulties when one is seeking to adjust to an alien environment. But once the initial period of adjustment is over, it is easier to acclimatise oneself.

Pause.

NORM: That's very true.

AHMED: Yes. Now if you'll excuse me, I'll...

NORM: Do you know what? You're insulting me, do you know that? Eh? You're insinuating that I'm some kind of drunken pervert.

AHMED: Oh no, you have misconstrued my actions. I think nothing of the kind.

NORM: Then why do you keep backing away, eh? Answer me that.

AHMED: Well... I mean... it's late. It's late at night.

NORM: I know it's late. That's no reason. You think you're a bit above me. You don't want to talk to me. I'm insulted. If you think I'm a drunken perv, why don't you say so? Why don't you come right out and say it?

AHMED: I'm very sorry if you think that. Perhaps I have shown bad manners. I offer my humble apologies.

NORM: Never been so insulted in all—

AHMED: Please! Believe me. I did not mean to be rude.

NORM: You sure?

AHMED: Of course I'm sure.

NORM: Well, all right then, don't worry about it. Just a bit of a misunderstanding, that's all. No hard feelings. Jees, I tell you what, Ahmed, you really looked scared there for a minute.

He laughs.

AHMED: [*smiling, relieved*] Did I really?

NORM: [*jovially*] Yeah, you were terrified. You looked as if a kick in the crutch and a cold frankfurt'd finish you off. You're all right now?

AHMED: Yes.

NORM: You sure?

AHMED: Yes.

NORM: No worries?

AHMED: No.

NORM: You sure?

AHMED: Yes.

NORM: Everything's fine?

AHMED: Yes.

Pause.

NORM: You sure?

AHMED: Yes! Yes! I am sure!

NORM: [*prowling around* AHMED] Good. I'm pleased to hear that. That's very encouraging. Where do you live, Ahmed?

AHMED: I am at La Perouse, not far from the university. I'm sharing a flat with some Indian students.

NORM: La Perouse, eh? What, right out at Botany Bay?

AHMED: Yes. The flat overlooks the bay.

NORM: That's where it all started, isn't it? That's where old Captain Cook landed, Botany Bay. Must have given the boongs a fright, eh? I mean, the Aborigines were probably quite surprised to see the white men in their big ships. All those sails in the wind. They probably thought the white man was some kind of monster.

AHMED: That's quite possible.

NORM: You know much about Australian history?

AHMED: No, not a great deal. I am studying it at the university.

NORM: You're out at the old brain-drainer, eh? What course would you be taking, Ahmed?

AHMED: Arts. I am studying for a Bachelor of Arts degree.

NORM: Arts, eh? What, bit of a painter, are you?

AHMED: No, I am not doing painting, I am studying the humanities.

NORM: Oh. Uh… now just what exactly would that involve, Ahmed?

AHMED: History, mainly. I am majoring in History.

NORM: Oh, History. Yeah, I see. I was never much good at History. No head for dates. That was my trouble. Tell me, Ahmed, what with your education and all, you'd be able to form a few impressions, like, of this country. I mean, you'd be able to sort a few things out. Have your own opinions.

AHMED: Yes, I have formed several opinions of your country… some good, others bad.

NORM: What would you say was a bad point, Ahmed?

AHMED: Well, I would rather talk about the good points. It would hardly be diplomatic on my part to seek to undermine—

NORM: Ar come on, Ahmed, don't give us that. Don't be a creamer all your life. Tell me a bad point. The White Australia Policy, the way we govern ourselves, anything you like. I want you to tell me, right here and now, what you feel, in your own mind, is a bad thing in this country.

AHMED: Well then, if you are so keen to hear my opinion, I would say that... uh... Well, for one thing, one of the, uh, less desirable aspects of your society, to my mind, would be the tendency of the mass media to be merely the mouthpiece of the big commercial and military interests... the, uh, free press, as it were. They brainwash the people. They... Oh, please forgive me, I forget myself. As I said, it is not perhaps my place to seek to condemn your country. I have my own opinion, but I do not go around broadcasting it as it would not be the diplomatic thing to do.

NORM: Well, that's fair enough, Ahmed. I can see your point of view. For instance, if I went over to Pakistan, I wouldn't tell you blokes how to run your country. I'd keep it to meself. I wouldn't throw me weight around in someone else's country. Mind you, I'd have me own opinion, though.

AHMED: Ah, that is quite right. I think you have put it most appositely, Norm. I have my own views but I observe a diplomatic silence.

NORM: That's a very sensible idea. I understand exactly how you must feel, Ahmed. When I was in Egypt during the war, I didn't think the Egyptians ran their country extra well. But I kept quiet, I didn't want to crool meself. And just between you and me and the garbage can, I didn't cotton much to the Egyptians themselves. We had our differences, I can tell you. I never took to them.

AHMED: A difficult race to understand, perhaps. I can readily appreciate the frustrations you must have experienced.

NORM: It's nice of you to say that, Ahmed, because these blokes were hard to understand. There were faults on both sides, of course, and there's two sides to every question, as you well know, but, well, there it is. I just didn't take to them. Might have been my fault. You see, they're a cunning lot, those Gyppos. Take you down as soon as look at you. Some of our blokes were easy pickings for those bastards. Fruit on the sideboard. That's what they were.

AHMED: How long were you over there?

NORM: Quite a while. During the desert campaign. I was in Tobruk, mate. I was one of the Rats of Tobruk.

AHMED: That was quite a battle, wasn't it?

NORM: Yes, it was a pretty good scrap—but we held out, mate, we stuck to our guns. We fought with everything we had—I even knocked one of 'em down with me bare hands. It's true. He was a prisoner, trying to escape, but I apprehended him and jobbed him one. I can still remember that night—I was out for a stroll on the gravel, savouring my last cigarette, when I heard this click in the moonlight, see. So I hid in the shadows and had a screw at the compound. [*Miming*] Then I saw him. It was a Kraut, cutting through the wires, trying to escape from us, the AIF. So I jumped out and confronted him… I offered to take him quietly, but the bastard come at me with a knife. I just stood there, cool as the proverbial cucumber. Then we started circling each other in the dark, round and round and round. [*Circling* AHMED] Then all of a sudden I grabbed him…

He grabs AHMED *by the throat.*

... and I—

He suddenly releases the struggling AHMED, *who breaks away and retreats a few paces, watching* NORM *warily.*

Jees, what have I done? Sorry, Ahmed, old mate. I got a bit carried away there for a minute. Are you all right?

AHMED: [*straightening his collar*] Uh... yes, I'm all right.

NORM: I just got too excited, Ahmed, and that's a fact. I hope you'll forgive me.

AHMED: [*not quite won over*] Oh, certainly.

NORM: You know how it is, you do your block, you don't know where you are. Sure you're all right?

AHMED: Quite sure.

NORM: What a thing to do! And you a visitor to this country. I don't know what you must think.

AHMED: Oh, don't worry about it, Norm. You got a little excited, that's all.

NORM: You'll probably go back to your country and tell 'em we're all a mob of savages out here.

AHMED: [*profusely*] Not at all, Norm, not at all. I will do nothing of the kind.

NORM: You'll go back there and spread the word that we're all barbarians out here.

AHMED: No, no, I will do no such thing.

NORM: Don't know what came over me.

AHMED: Believe me, Norm, it's all right. No harm has been done.

NORM: You'll forgive me, then?

AHMED: Of course, of course.

> NORM *looks at him, smiles and pats him on the back.*

NORM: Good on you, Ahmed, old mate. You're a good sport. Here, have a cigarette.

> *He offers a packet.*

AHMED: Thank you.

> AHMED *takes a cigarette and puts it in his mouth. He fumbles in his pocket for matches.* NORM *brings out his cigarette lighter and flicks it on.* AHMED *leans over to light his cigarette, but stops a few inches short of the lighter. He looks at the burning flame and then takes the cigarette out of his mouth and looks at* NORM, *who is beaming benignly at him. He looks at the flame again, hesitates, then finally puts the cigarette in his mouth and lights it from the flame.*

NORM: Anyway, Ahmed, as I was telling you, I floored this bloody Kraut. Really laid him out. He was all over the place like a mad woman's lunchbox. just lying there waiting for me to kill him. But do you know what I did?

AHMED: No, Norm, I have no idea.

NORM: I spared him. That's what I did. I could never kill a man in cold blood, Ahmed. It's not in my code of ethics. Not what I call doing the right thing. Human life is sacred, Ahmed, that's my firm belief. So I took him back to the compound and handed him over to the proper authorities without laying a hand on him. I was the hero of the whole battalion after that little effort, I can tell you. I was the toast of Tobruk, and that's the gospel truth. You do believe me, don't you?

AHMED: Why, of course, Norm.

NORM: It's as true as I'm standing here. And if I tell a lie, then may the Good Lord strike me down from above with a bolt from the blue.

He darts an anxious glance upwards.

AHMED: That's very interesting, Norm. But don't you feel that despite your heroic act, the barbarity of war left a scar on you?

NORM: Not a scratch. Of course, I was lucky, luckier than my old man. He was in the Gallipoli campaign, one of the original Anzacs. [*Pause.*] He fell at Lone Pine. [*Pause.*] It was a dawn raid. He was killed by a stray bullet. They buried him the same morning.

AHMED: I'm very sorry to hear that.

NORM: Well, that's the way it goes. After all, the price of liberty is eternal vigilance.

AHMED: The price of what?

NORM: Liberty.

AHMED: Oh.

Pause.

NORM: You're not having a go at me, are you?

AHMED: No, not at all. I feel sorry for the Anzacs, poor fellows. However, the Anzac legend is often invoked in support of… other campaigns. But, forgive me, I am once again posing as a critic of your country. I must again remember that I am a visitor to this land. A thousand apologies.

NORM: That's all right, Ahmed. You've got your views and I

respect them. Long as you do the right thing by yourself and other blokes and don't go throwing your weight around, you'll be all right out here.

AHMED: Thank you, Norm, that is very good advice.

NORM: Don't mention it, Ahmed. I like to see blokes like you getting on well out here. All you Asian students coming out here to study and then going back to your own countries, it's a good thing, I reckon. Should be more of it. Mind you, though, not everyone goes along with it. A bloke at work said he didn't see the point of bringing a whole lot of boongs out here. Excuse the term, Ahmed, I'm just giving you a verbatim report, like, of what the bloke at work said. But I had occasion to take him to task when I heard him say that, Ahmed. I said, 'We're forging the bonds of friendship with our Asian neighbours. Knowledge is the key to the door of understanding and friendship', that's what I told him.

AHMED: That's very interesting Norm. But what specific course does this understanding and friendship take?

NORM: Well, you know... understanding... and... being friendly.

AHMED: I see.

NORM: [*quickly*] Anyway, Ahmed, what do you do in your spare time? Got any hobbies, play any sport?

AHMED: No, I don't really have time for that sort of thing.

NORM: No time for sport? Jees, that's a sad state of affairs. I always used to find time to play sport when I was a young feller. I used to play football before the war. Rugby League. I played lock. That was my position, lock. Talk about cover defence! I used to hit 'em hard and low, round the knees, down they went. They can't run without legs, can they? That was my philosophy. But I was always a clean player, Ahmed, I never put the boot in. Always played hard and clean, I was a good sportsman, too. Never sold the dump to a mate. I always played fair, but if they ever mucked me about, biff! Send for the cleaners. All over bar the shouting. Know what I mean? I remember one bloke. A real coot. Played prop for Balmain Juniors. Tall bloke, he was. A long, thin streak of pelican shit. He tried to hang one on me at Leichhardt Oval once, so I administered a knuckle sandwich to him. He woke up in Our Lady of Mercy Hospital. Should have known better; I always observed the true spirit of the game. Ever played Rugby League, Ahmed?

AHMED: No, unfortunately. I have to spend most of my time studying.

NORM: That's a pity. It's not healthy, you know, to keep your nose stuck in a book all the time.

AHMED: Oh, I don't spend all my time studying. I am compelled to work at night to put myself through university.

NORM: Yeah? Why doesn't your old man send you a few bob to help you along? You wouldn't have to flog your chops too much then.

AHMED: My father is unable to supply me with financial assistance because he, unlike some other people, is not very affluent.

NORM: Jees, that's a bit rough. You've got my sympathy, Ahmed. You must have a pretty tough job, having to work and study at the same time.

AHMED: It is not easy.

NORM: What are you going to do when you finish?

AHMED: When I obtain my degree I intend to return to Pakistan and attempt to render assistance to the under-privileged peoples, perhaps also to undermine the position of the over-privileged peoples. I have some old school friends over there who are dedicated to the cause. I remember when I graduated from secondary school in Pakistan we had a speech day at the end of the year. It was an official ceremony, too, with all the, er, dignitaries, as you say out here. All the top civil servants and military men and businessmen were there on the official dais with the school authorities. As the highlight of the occasion it was arranged that a flock of doves would be released by the big window and would fly out over the playing fields of the school as some sort of symbolic gesture. But unfortunately they took fright at all the lights and the applause and suffered severe indigestion. They flew round and round and round above the dignitaries, bestowing excrement on the Establishment. We all laughed and laughed and some of the boys threw paper darts at the dignitaries. When one boy introduced a fire hose into the proceedings, the situation grew somewhat out of hand. I shall always cherish the memory I have of one bespattered military gentleman crawling around under a table trying to find one of his medals, as the gentle rain from heaven fell all around him. We boys had a great time. It was a mad, wild, exhilarating day, I shall always remember it.

> NORM *has been sitting on the handrail during this speech.*
> *Now he stands.*

NORM: Yeah, it sounds like a real rort. But, if you don't mind my saying so, Ahmed, in a spirit of friendly criticism, with no malice of forethought, or any offence intended on my part, don't you think your behaviour was a bit on the rough side? I mean, you know, I'd be the last bloke to start defending the bloody dignitaries, and I don't go much on pomp and circumstance and all that sort of garbage, but still, all in all, and looking at both sides of the question, I'd be a bit inclined to say that the blokes who get into these official positions, well, they're pretty important blokes, and I'd say they deserve a little bit of respect from the general public. I mean, I'd be the last one to start putting them up on a pedestal, and if they ever bung on side with me, mate, they know what they can expect. I don't take no crap from no one. But, by the same token, and taking all things into consideration, I reckon that if a bloke's in an official capacity, like those blokes who came to your school, well, it's only fair that he should earn a little bit of respect.

AHMED: I fear I must disagree with you there, Norm. I do not regard these accursed officials with perhaps the same reverence as you do. We shall overthrow them! We demand social justice! Oh, I beg your pardon, Norm, I fear I was carried away there for a moment. I hope you will excuse my excessive zeal.

NORM: Ar, she's right, Ahmed. But just remember what I said. Anyway, I hope you get through uni all right, so you can go back to your country and do whatever it is you want to do. As a matter of fact, I've got a son at uni. Young Bernie. He's studying in America. He's at the MIT—the Massachusetts Institute of Technology.

AHMED: What's he studying?

NORM: Well… technology, you know? He's got an assured

future in front of him, my Bernie, he'll be a leader in science and industry—he's got the qualifications, you see. He's a real cluey bloke, no risk. We were very proud of him when he graduated from Sydney Uni. It was an official ceremony. All the dignitaries were there... the Governor, the Premier and the Governor-General, all up there on the official dais with all the other authorities. What a magnificent sight! Bernie wasn't nervous. He came through fine. It was a very impressive ceremony.

AHMED: It must have been a proud moment for you, Norm.

NORM: Yes, it certainly was. Bernie's the only one in our family with a university degree. None of the rest of us are all that bright. But the Gallaghers are getting on, mate. My old man was a factory worker, I'm a white-collar worker, and now Bernie's a technologist. Things are looking up, I tell you.

AHMED: What kind of white-collar work do you do, Norm?

NORM: Well, er, actually I'm a storeman, like, in a warehouse. But I wear a white shirt and tie under me dustcoat, though. I mean, I'm not sort of technically a white-collar worker, but I wear a white collar, y'see? I mean, there's a bit of a fine distinction involved in this. Y'see, I'm not always in the warehouse—I spend a lot of time in the office, checking invoices and rectifying a few anomalies.

AHMED: Ah, I see. It sounds very complicated.

NORM: Yes, it's a funny business. But I'm doing all right for meself. Making a bit of money, got a nice big house, everything laid on, I'm doing fine. But there's just one thing wrong, Ahmed.

AHMED: What's that?

NORM: Well, you see, Ahmed, I'm all alone now, since my good
wife Beryl passed away to the heavens above.

AHMED: I'm very sorry to hear that, Norm, you must be rather
lonely.

NORM: That I am, Ahmed, that I am. Sometimes when I'm out
in the backyard, watering the frangipanis, I feel very lonely,
I really do. Now that dear Beryl's in another world I don't
know where I am. She was a lovely woman, a real beauty in
her day, jet-black hair, sparkling eyes, and an ear for music.
Played a good game of bowls in her twilight years. But now
she's gone and where am I? Up the creek without a paddle!
It's the good times I miss, Ahmed, those magic moments
that make life seem worthwhile. Like the time we danced all
night at the Bronte RSL. Yes, I really miss dear old Beryl,
with her happy laugh, her way with kids, her curried eggs on
toast of a winter's night. But now, Ahmed, now I sit at home
alone and think of yesteryear.

AHMED: That is most unfortunate, Norm. But surely you must
have some human contact, some form of social intercourse?

NORM: Oh yeah, my daughter Lorraine comes round and cooks
me roast dinner of a Sunday. But she's married, you see, she's
got her own life to lead. She made a good catch, that girl. Got
on to a real go-ahead type. Young Gary. He's in the retail
business, you know. Runs a hot dog stand at Harold Park.
Got his eye on a kiosk at Miranda. No flies on Gary, mate,
you mark my words. Fine-looking young feller, too. Very
tall, with big broad shoulders and a good head for figures.
Likes a dash of lemon in his Resch's. He comes around and
takes me out to the football sometimes. I get a little lonely,
you see, being all alone. I like to get out and do something,

meet some people. I like to have a nice chat with a bloke, find out how he's getting on in the world. A bloke like you, for instance, Ahmed. A visitor to our shores. A young citizen from the south-east Asian sub-continent.

AHMED: Well... I hope I can... I mean... if I can be of... any... that is, I...

NORM: Step over here a minute, will you?

Pause.

AHMED: What?

They look at each other.

NORM: Just step over here for a minute.

Pause.

AHMED: Why?

NORM: What's the matter, Ahmed? Come here.

AHMED *moves warily closer to* NORM.

Over here. Under the light.

AHMED *moves closer.*

AHMED: What do you want?

NORM *surveys* AHMED.

NORM: Just as I thought. [*Pause.*] You haven't really got such a dark skin, have you?

AHMED: A dark skin? What do you mean?

NORM: I mean you're not a black, are you? You could pass for a Greek or a Turk. You've got more of an olive complexion.

AHMED: What are you getting at? I fail to understand...

NORM *laughs. He moves out from the shadows.*

NORM: Don't get upset, Ahmed. Don't do your block. I was only thinking that if you didn't have a dark skin you'd be all right. I mean, it'd be all right for you to stay here, like, get a job and stay in this country. But you haven't really got a dark skin, have you? It's sort of olive coloured. They'd never call you 'Mr Midnight', would they?

AHMED: Some would.

NORM: Eh, come on Ahmed, now don't have a wetty. No offence meant. You're not angry, are you? Eh?

AHMED: No, it's all right, Norm, I'm not offended.

NORM: Good. We're still mates, then. I suppose you'd have a right to get touchy about that sort of thing. I wouldn't blame you for getting touchy. I can see your point of view.

AHMED: Thank you, Norm. I appreciate your concern.

NORM: She's right, Ahmed. I tell you what, in this world we've got to learn to understand the problems of others and not worry too much about our own.

AHMED: That is very true, Norm. You seem to possess a most humanitarian outlook on life.

NORM: I'm very flattered, Ahmed, to hear you say that. In this world there's too many blokes getting in for their chop and not worrying about their mates. You'd appreciate that, I mean, being a historian and all.

AHMED: Uh, yes, I suppose I would.

NORM: You know, as I was saying, Ahmed, you could do all right for yourself if you stayed out here. After you got your degree, you could stay here and be a useful asset. I mean, as I said, you're not really black, so you wouldn't have that much trouble.

AHMED: Well, perhaps. I shall have to obtain my degree before I consider a proposal of that nature.

NORM: That's fair enough. First things first, after all. But give it a bit of thought, Ahmed. You'd be welcome out here, I can vouch for that. The people'd treat you just like one of their own, no risk. You'd be all right. No worries there. You could make your way in the world out here.

AHMED: Yes, it is a most attractive proposition.

NORM: You could have a good time out here, Ahmed. It's an easy life. Take this morning, for instance. On Sunday mornings I sit out on the terrace and sip a Tia Maria and read the sports section. Lorraine's in the kitchen, smell of a roast lamb on the breeze, what more could you want? Green lawns all around, vista of the harbour, Holden in the garage, I'm sweet. No worries. See what I'm getting at? You wouldn't have that in Pakistan, now would you? You could set yourself up very nicely out here. There's lots to recommend it, believe you me. It's a bloody good set-up, take my tip. Look at me. I've got a good job, good pay—I'm doing all right. A reliable firm, nice personnel. You know who I had a beer with on Friday?

AHMED: No, Norm, I have no idea. Who?

NORM: I had a beer with the man himself, the Managing Director, my boss. [*Filled with awe*] I drank with the Managing Director of the firm.

AHMED: That must have been… an experience.

NORM: He shouted a round, too, just like any ordinary bloke

would. He took a shine to me, too, I could see that. He was very impressed with me. It was a most cordial affair. I know how to conduct meself on these occasions. Not like my old man. Do you know what he had?

AHMED: What?

NORM: He had a criminal record. It's true. My mother told me. He was put away for a while.

AHMED: What did he do?

NORM: He bashed up his boss. Yes, that's right, bashed up his boss. It's… inconceivable, that's what it is. Talk about a blot on the family record. It's a stain on the Gallagher escutcheon. The memory of it still haunts me. It's enough to make you want to chuck, isn't it? 'Course you wouldn't find that sort of thing around these days. Rare as a pregnant nun. That's progress for you. We've cut that sort of thing out.

AHMED: Yes, it would indeed be a rare occurrence in contemporary times.

NORM: Too right. Yes, he was a real ratbag, my old man. Mad Dan Gallagher, they used to call him. Always getting into fights and organising strikes and things. He died just before I was born. My mother nearly had a miscarriage when she heard the news, but she got over it all right. I arrived safe and sound. She used to tell me about him when I was a young feller. He was always holding meetings in our living room. Then they'd all go into the kitchen and my mother would make them a cup of tea. All big men they were, with horny hands and sturdy braces. My mother was real tiny. They'd pick her up and whirl her round and round and round the room and when they were drunk they'd sing 'I'll Take You

Home Again, Kathleen' or 'The Wild Colonial Boy'. There was a whole mob of them—Flanigan, Hanigan, Branigan, Lanigan, O'Toole, O'Riley and Schultz. Then one night the cops raided the place and took them away. They were all singing 'Sweet Adeline' in the black maria. What a bunch of ratbags they were! Some of them used to come round after the war to see my mother. I was only a kid then. They gave me some liquorice. We lost touch with them after a while. It was a bit before my time, all that. I got dim memories... like... long time ago... bit cloudy... Wobbly bastards!

NORM *kicks over the garbage can in a fit of anger.* AHMED *is a bit startled, but doesn't move.*

Jees, there I go again, doing me block. Excuse me, Ahmed, but my old man does make me angry. He had no respect for law and order and common decency.

AHMED: Perhaps it is sometimes desirable to effect an alteration in the status quo.

NORM: Could be. But my old man wanted to change things, Ahmed, he tried to buck the system. You can't do that.

AHMED: Not in this country, at any rate.

NORM: No fear. Anyway, they got onto him pretty quick. The policemen came around and took him away, but not before he'd bashed one of them up. An officer of the law. Disgraceful! It's like I told you, he had no respect for law and order, and that's a terrible thing.

AHMED: Oh, I don't know, sometimes I feel the police deserve some form of retaliation from their victims.

NORM: Ar, come on, Ahmed, give the copper a fair go. They're not such bad blokes. Give them a break. They're just doing their job, that's all. They only want to preserve law and order in the community. Mind you, though, if a mug copper ever started pushing me around, I'd job him good and proper, no risk about that. I don't take no crap from no one. But, by the same token, Ahmed, I reckon our policemen are doing a pretty good job and I'd do all that's in my power, all that's humanly possible, to assist them in the performance of their duties. Go easy on the old wallopers, that's what I say, give the coppers a fair go.

AHMED: Well, I think they get a pretty fair go. I observed one beating up an old drunk earlier this evening. For no reason, either. It was sheer brutality.

NORM: Now come on, Ahmed, the policemen do a good job keeping all the drunks and pervs off the streets and making them safe for decent citizens. These blokes are a menace, you know, especially the pervs. Ever been solicited, Ahmed?

AHMED: No, I have not been accorded that distinction.

NORM: Well, you want to watch out for that sort of thing. It could happen any time.

AHMED: Yes, I'm certain it could.

NORM: Yes, any time, any time at all. Pervs aren't choosy, you know. Some of these blokes'll drop their tweeds for a ripe banana. I saw an old perv in Centennial Park last week. He was having a tug in the gutter, going at it hammer and tongs. He must have been hard up, eh?

AHMED: Uh… yes.

NORM: You ever get like that, Ahmed? Eh? Do you?

AHMED: No.

NORM: Never get hard up?

AHMED: No.

NORM: Never had a tug in the gutter?

AHMED: Certainly not. I hardly think a public thoroughfare is a suitable venue for con-ducting autonomous experiments of that nature.

Pause.

NORM: You got a funny way of putting things, Ahmed.

AHMED: You find my syntax humorous?

NORM: No, not humorous, Ahmed. Just funny. I suppose you get a lot of people who admit you speak better than they do, eh? I bet a lot of people say you speak better than the average native-born Australian.

AHMED: Yes, I have been paid that compliment.

NORM: Yes, I could very well… envisage that. But anyway, Ahmed, that's just another reason why you should settle down out here—there's no language barrier. You could live here very… autonomously. You're not like all those chows down in Dixon Street that jabber away in Chinese half the time. You can speak the Queen's English. You know, you could really make something of yourself if you stayed out here, Ahmed. Look at my boss, for instance.

AHMED: That Managing Director fellow?

NORM: Yes. He was telling me about the struggles he's had to establish his great enterprise. It wasn't easy, he said, in the early days. It was hard at first, but he won through in the end. It was a stirring struggle, but one man's dream came true. He became a legend in his own lifetime. He challenged the gods and carved out a name for himself that will survive in the annals of human endeavour. But that's the sort of thing that happens in this country, Ahmed. You could have a success story like that, you know. Start off with a billycart and finish up with a fleet of Boeing 727s.

AHMED: Perhaps. I have not given much thought to—

NORM: You could settle down, get a house in a nice suburb with lots of trees and birds and things. A place where you can wash the car of a Saturday and do a bit of gardening of a Sunday. Do you like gardening, Ahmed?

AHMED: It is indeed a pleasant pastime. I like to—

NORM: That's for sure. There's nothing I like better than to get out in the garden of a Sunday. Put me amongst the hydrangeas and I'm at peace with the world. When there's a breeze in the palms and the sun's getting low, I get out in the yard and get stuck into the weeds. I weed away to my heart's content. I couldn't ask for any more in this world or the next, and that's my solemn oath. It's the simple pleasures, Ahmed, that make this life worth living. Sometimes when I'm on my way home from church of a Sunday night, when the strains of the last hymn have died and the humble pilgrims have gone home to bed, I stop and look up at the stars in the sky and think what a wonderful world it is we live in. But, by the same token, Ahmed, I do miss the old days a bit. The times when we used to sit around the fire with our friends and sing all night. There was real warmth between people in those days. We were like brothers, all getting stuck into the grog together. And when I was out in the bush and I stopped at a pub, I knew every bloke in the place within five minutes. Community feeling, that's what it was; community feeling. We used to have it in the old days. And when I sit home of a night, all by myself,

I open a can of DA and think back over my life. The happy, happy times, like when the young fellers started calling on Lorraine. She was a lovely girl. Dead spit of Beryl, she was. She—ar jees, Ahmed, look, I'm sorry to carry on like this. I don't know what you must think.

AHMED: Oh, no, Norm, you go right ahead.

NORM: Sorry to crap on so much, Ahmed. I don't know what came over me. It's just that I don't get much of a chance to talk to people these days. And I do like a bit of a yarn, I really do. Just to talk to someone, that's all I want. And when I do find someone to talk to, I just mag away like an old woman and ruin everything.

AHMED: You say whatever you want to, Norm, I don't mind.

NORM: I just crap on and spoil it all.

AHMED: No you don't, Norm. I have been listening, believe me.

NORM: You mean that, Ahmed?

AHMED: Of course I mean it.

NORM: Good on you, Ahmed, you're a real human being. I don't suppose it's easy to put up with an old bludger like me.

AHMED: On the contrary, Norm, it has been most interesting to meet you.

NORM: Thanks, old mate, that's very nice of you, to say that. Well, I'd better let you go now, Ahmed. But just before you go, I would like to say this from the very bottom of my heart, that I wish you every success in the world. And I do hope you get on well out here. Now you're sure you're settling down all right?

AHMED: Oh yes, I'm making my way.

NORM: I'm glad to hear it, Ahmed. I wouldn't like to think of you as being lonely. You see, I'm on my own, too, and I know what it's like. A young bloke your age ought to be out and about, mixing with people, getting amongst the girls. You know what your trouble is, Ahmed, don't you?

AHMED: What?

NORM: You're too shy. That's the first thing I noticed about you. You're too shy.

AHMED: You think so?

NORM: Of course. It's obvious.

AHMED: It is true that I do not have many friends.

NORM: Look, I tell you what, Ahmed. Why don't you go up to the New South Wales Leagues Club and have a good time. Mention my name to the bloke on the door and you'll be in like the proverbial Flynn. Just tell 'em Norm sent you, that's all you have to do. Go up with your mates and get on the hops. You'll soon get to know the blokes up there. A great mob they are, too. I've got a feeling they'll take to you, Ahmed, I think you'll go down well.

AHMED: Thank you, Norm, I shall bear that in mind.

NORM: You do that, Ahmed, you do that. I'd like to see you meeting some people, making some friends. Loneliness is a terrible curse, Ahmed, and I'd like to see you coming out of your shell. We're not such a bad mob out here, you know. We might be a bit on the rough-and-ready side, but our heart's in the right place.

AHMED: Oh, I have had ample proof of that.

NORM: And as I said, Ahmed, you really ought to give a thought to staying out here. Find yourself a good woman, something more than just a weekend root, and settle down and raise a family. Buy a weekender on the coast, join the local leagues club—ever been to a leagues club, Ahmed?

AHMED: No, I have that pleasure in front of me.

NORM: Fabulous places. They've improved a lot, these clubs. Twenty years ago they weren't much chop, just a place to go when you wanted to get out on the grog. But now, jees, what a difference! They go in for amenities a lot these days, for the comfort of the patrons. They're very well-appointed, these clubs, very well-appointed. Anyway, Ahmed, there it is. Good prospects, you could have a good time, what more could you ask for? This place'd be made for a bloke like you.

AHMED: Well, I think I will concentrate on completing my tertiary education first. My primary concern is to obtain a liberal education and my secondary concern is to gain a deeper understanding of human behaviour.

NORM: Ah… yes, that's fair enough. But keep it in mind, Ahmed, we'd love to have you. And the people—they'd take you to their hearts. Everyone from Alice Springs to breakfast time. It'll be a red carpet job.

AHMED: Thank you very much, Norm, that is very nice of you. I must say I have received some warm hospitality from a lot of people since I have been in your country. It has been most gratifying. Of course, uh, not everyone has extended this hospitality towards visitors from eastern backgrounds, such as myself.

NORM: Ar well, you've got to take the rough with the smooth. There's ratbags wherever you go. But the majority of people'll do the right thing. I think you'll go down well out here.

AHMED: Thank you again, Norm. I certainly hope so. You have given me something to think about.

NORM: Glad to hear it. Well, Ahmed, I must say it's been a pleasure to meet you and have this little talk. I mean, to reach a common understanding. That's what the world needs, I reckon, a bit of common understanding.

AHMED: That is very true. I have enjoyed meeting you, too, Norm, it has been a real pleasure.

NORM: Put 'er there, mate.

He offers his hand.

AHMED: [*reaching out to shake hands*] Yes, I—

> NORM *punches* AHMED *in the stomach, then in the face. He grabs* AHMED*'s head and bashes it against the post. Then he flings the limp body over the handrail.*

NORM: Fuckin' boong.

The clock strikes one.

Blackout.

THE END

THE FAILED NATIONALISM OF ALEX BUZO

Stephen Sewell

Nationalist movements, wherever they are, find a sense of identity in the language of the group trying to unify itself. Nation building is very much a question of language creation and celebration, with poets and playwrights always at the forefront of the process, and this is as true of the invention of Hebrew as it was of Poland's attempt to overthrow Russian domination in the 19th Century,[1] or England's rise and transformation of itself into Britain under Elizabeth I, with the works of Shakespeare and Marlowe thrilling audiences not only with uplifting versions of their history, but with the power of their language. The ebb and flow of Australian nationalism has similarly been accompanied by eruptions of myth and language making, from the time of the Bulletin bush poets, Banjo Paterson and Henry Lawson, amongst others, through to the chaotic period following the Second World War when, as the United States replaced Britain as the pole of our national politics, there was a short space of time offering the promise of independence that was quickly occupied by writers such as Dorothy Hewett and Frank Hardy, once again celebrating a rough-edged Australian vernacular against the official English championed by the upholders of taste and the status quo.

This restless yearning for Australian independence re-emerged in the sixties as Australia was again drawn into another war not of its choosing, and for the first time in our history conscripts were to be sent to fight people in their own homeland in a place called Vietnam. Conscripts landed at Nui Dat in 1966 and the first conscript died there a few days later,[2] sparking an anti-war movement that within four years was threatening the hegemony of the Liberal-National Party that had governed Australia throughout the entire post-war period. By 1970, the various oppositional forces—political, religious, cultural— had coalesced into the formidable Vietnam Moratorium Campaign which was able to mount demonstrations of 100,000 people in Melbourne alone, and 200,000 people nationwide. And that same year, the Australian Performing Group, which had been gestating in Melbourne's *La Mama,* was formed—a theatre group *"influenced by the new politics of that era, (that) wanted ... to be political in a way that the conventional bourgeois theatre in Australia certainly wasn't",[3]* but all dedicated to putting the Australian language onstage. Alex Buzo's *Norm and Ahmed* was one of the first plays performed.

Language is and remained Buzo's central concern. The tough, violent, sinuous vernacular filled with Australian history but somehow ignorant of it. Like all great writers, Buzo loved the cadences and rhythm of his own language, and thrilled to his virtuosity with it. *"Yes, he was a real ratbag, my old man. Mad Dan Gallagher ..."*, Norm says, relishing the words as they tumble forth. Later he tells Ahmed, *"Sometimes when I'm out in the backyard, watering the frangipanis, I feel very lonely, I really do ..."* and the menacing poetry entrances us as much as it does the hapless Pakistani who has had the misfortune to fall into the web of the darkly malevolent stranger.

Norm and Ahmed, two liminal figures of Australia's imagination: one the primal father, a Tobruk veteran and son of an Anzac—or so he says[4]—a figure loved and loathed by generations who had lived under his baleful eye as he punished them for the punishment he had received in our endless wars; the other a visitor from a half-imagined future, polite, educated, thoughtful and inevitably doomed at the hands of the castrating tormentor he happens to meet like an evil spirit at midnight.

Like a bad son, Buzo delights in teasing out the contradictions of his monstrous creation. Norm is alternately threatening and seductive, foul-mouthed and genteel, a conformist bully who thinks the coppers deserve "a fair go" but whose opponents, the "wobbly"[5] unionists, deserve a kicking because you "can't buck the system". Norm is very much a father figure, one that confronted anti-war protestors on the streets of Australia and who, in the form of the RSL, had already had

Alan Seymour's play about Anzac Day, *The One Day of the Year*, banned from the inaugural Adelaide Festival in 1960, thus ensuring its instant success. But it is not so much satire, or even political commentary, that Buzo is interested in while unleashing Norm on the stage, as the sheer inventiveness and audacity of his language. *"That was my position, lock. Talk about cover defence! I used to hit 'em hard and low, round the knees, down they went."* And a little later, *"I remember one bloke. A real coot...Tall bloke he was. A long, thin streak of pelican shit."* And on and on through all the delights of Australian slang. *Perv ... creamer ... Gyppos ... easy pickings ...flog your chops ...* gems of a colourful language spill effortlessly from Norm's voluble mouth. Buzo was not himself working class, but had a fascination with the rough, muscular language of working class people, so his play bustles with the dark, filthy poetry of the demimonde. *"You looked as if a kick in the crutch and a cold frankfurt'd finish you off"*, he says to Ahmed soon after their meeting; and later, *"I floored this bloody kraut. Really laid him out. He was all over the place like a mad woman's lunchbox"*. This was the argot that soon made the prison playwright, Jim McNeil, famous, leading to his early release and catastrophic decline, and it was an argot that was vital, potent, angry and most importantly, *Australian*. Because for the people championing it, both the theatre-makers and the audience they attracted, *that* was the most important thing. That we were hearing *our stories* told *our way* in *our language*.

And language was what drove it. It heralded a new era when the Australian stage would be a platform for Australian voices, and so suited the times of change that were sweeping not only Australia but the world, culminating here with the election of the Whitlam Labor Government, the end of conscription and our involvement in the American war against Vietnam,[6] the unleashing of a reform program that was met almost instantly with an hysterical backlash from the institutional powers which had come to see themselves as the natural rulers of the country, a backlash leading to the constitutional coup of 1975 and Labor's loss of government in the subsequent electoral debacle when the Murdoch press pulled out all stops to ensure its defeat.[7] The experiment was over, and with it the fire that had burnt in the bellies of the cultural leaders, so closely allied and identified with Whitlam's challenge. But that was still in the future when *Norm and Ahmed* premiered at the Pram[8] in 1970, and in that moment it was the working class that was in the ascendant, slowly gathering strength to declare '*It's Time'*[9] two years later. It might seem strange to describe the brutal thuggish racist, Norm, as a working-class hero, but his centrality on the stage of Buzo's play betrayed the grim fascination a largely tertiary-educated audience had for its working class forebears, brutes and killers who had taken this land and subdued it with a horrific violence that is still only grudgingly acknowledged, if at all, and more often than not denied. Norm was the Australia the new generation was confronting and struggling with to wrestle a future for themselves, and one hopefully that was able to deal with some of his crimes,[10] indicated so arrestingly in his verbal forays. And his final, sickening assault. This was a man whose endearing sentimentality camouflaged a blindly hateful savagery and who is, at heart, a psychotic killer who tips an unconscious and possibly already dead stranger over a handrail snarling, *"Fucking boong"* after tricking him into accepting his hand of friendship. A dangerous man, in other words, who is nevertheless our hero.

This was what Australian men were, before the seventies' resurgence of feminism hit,[11] and what our model of masculinity was; and we find him again and again in the literature of the time, in Williamson's *Removalists* (1971, La Mama), Romeril's *Floating World* (1975, Australian Performing Group) and even Hibberd's *Stretch of the Imagination* (1972, Australian Performing Group) where the irascible Monk O'Neil rants, *"it's as cold as a cunt on concrete."* The same man, alternately kindly and friendly or foul-mouthed and murderously cruel, stalked Australia's dreams amusing and terrifying in equal measure until the working class ceased to be of interest, and those hard men were replaced once more by middle-class concerns expressed with wit and easy charm in a world apparently far removed from factories and shipyards and abattoirs. A world, that is to say, of angry people being ground down by relentless tyranny while their betters got on with making money and having affairs.

But to raise the question of who working people are actually working *for* is to raise one of the most difficult questions of a self-declared egalitarian state; is to raise, in other words, a *political* question, and while Buzo and his fellow playwrights were clearly writing, at this time, within a highly politicised environment, their interests were not, by and large, explicitly political.[12] Thus we have the irony that while *Norm and Ahmed* depicts a racist assault on a Pakistani student, it is not *about* racism, and consequently offers no analysis of Australian racism. Norm is merely a prejudiced bigot, an object of fear and derision. If Buzo has a lesson for us, it is not to be like Norm. We have no clues about what fuels Norm's anger and violence, or the real source of his fury; he is simply presented as an enigmatic force of nature, a dangerous animal that needs to be respected and perhaps admired from a distance, hence the dramaturgical question that every production faces: at what point does Norm decide to attack Ahmed? A question that really begs the question of whether Norm is capable of deciding anything, because really he is just an irrational force wrapped in a human skin; a monster that Ahmed mistakes for a man, our very own Caliban.

And who is Ahmed, anyhow? According to Bob Ellis,[13] the story of *Norm and Ahmed* came to Buzo from an incident involving a Pakistani friend, Mohammed Kazim, who was similarly menaced in a pub, but there is very little character detail in Ahmed's portrayal to give us any real sense of authenticity. Ahmed is more a cypher, a probe used to explore Norm, or rather, give Norm the opportunity to talk, and pounce. He is the tasty morsel Buzo dangles in front of the deadly Norm to get him to perform, and the decision by Jim Sharman in his premiere production[14] in Sydney[15] to black-up a white actor[16] rather than use a Pakistani one merely underlines the fantasy element of the role. Ahmed is an imagined Other to Norm's all-too-immediate Real. Ahmed is us, or perhaps Buzo himself, cool, detached, slyly judgmental and absolutely fascinated. And unable to tear his gaze away till the long-feared but totally inevitable barrage of blows makes escape impossible.

But while acting out a perverse Oedipal fantasy is certainly one element of *Norm and Ahmed*, as it was also on the streets outside in those tumultuous years of inter-generational conflict, it did not do much to illuminate the underlying issues behind so much discord or point to a possible solution, but to dismiss it in those terms would be as fatuous as to dismiss the anti-war revolt that gripped the world at the time as merely the tantrum of an over-privileged middle class.[17] For *Norm and Ahmed* is not a critical assault on a dinosaur lumbering its way to a well-deserved end, nor even a vaguely forgiving whinge about the blue-uniformed troglodytes breaking heads in George Street. What it is finally, and subtly, is a celebration—a bracing celebration of what it apparently condemns, and the last image we are left with is of Norm triumphant, bare-knuckled and panting, the inner demon of Australian nationhood revealed in all his virile impotency; sad, perhaps, but still there, fighting and victorious, and the embodiment of the only genuine character Australia has to offer. There is no question that Norm is the one we remember, and the one whose witticisms and ockerisms we repeat in the pub afterwards, emboldened and playfully trying on his persona to see how it fits, and often finding it fits rather too well. But if Sylvia Plath is right in saying that *"Every woman adores a Fascist, The boot in the face, the brute Brute heart of a brute like you"*,[18] she at least left us with the hope of our own survival as she concluded, *"There's a stake in your fat black heart, And the villagers never liked you ... Daddy, daddy, you bastard, I'm through"*, but Buzo offers no such solace. If every woman loves a fascist, so it seems does every Australian—and another thing we seem to love is defeat. Norm wins, and the Oedipal crisis is resolved not with the child's successful passing into adulthood, but rather his complete annihilation, perhaps anticipating the slap down of the Whitlam Government and the return to order in subsequent years; and it's here, in this strangely reactionary resolution, that we can see the real weakness of that nationalism of which Buzo was one of the brightest standard-bearers. For while Nixon and Kissinger were fearful revolution was knocking on their door, not many other people were, and even fewer in Australia, and while hundreds of thousands protested and sang 'We Shall Overcome' as the batons rained down, few believed that power could actually be seized and the new world about which they dreamt turned into a reality. The reality, as Buzo depicted, was Norm, waiting to put out a friendly hand and punch the living daylights out of you.

And so he did. The Australian left never recovered from the Whitlam coup. By the time the ALP returned to power, under Hawke in 1983, it was a very different beast with a very different agenda, and within months he was in the United States assuring Ronald Reagan of *"the fundamental importance that we in the new Labor government attach to the relationship with the United States"*.[19] The nationalist experiment was over and Australia was now firmly back in the fold. That same year, the Australian Performing Group closed shop and entered history as the epicentre, together with the Nimrod in Sydney, of the New Wave of playwriting that had produced Buzo, Williamson, Hibberd, Barry Oakley and John Romeril amongst others. The puff had gone out of the nationalist cause and by the time Bob Hawke was shaking Ronald Reagan's hand, Buzo was already writing about the language-mangling antics of sports journalists and handing out his annual Tautology Pennant, usually to football commentator Rex Mossop. The heyday was over, and the hard, angry language that had thrilled audiences had been replaced by pedantry, banter and repartee. And the nationalist cause was taken up by the monarchist, John Howard, and hitched once more to the Anzac legend and notions of patriotic duty.

Critical nationalism, subversive nationalism, nationalism looking to walk an independent road toward a future we chose ourselves, was dead, and what had replaced it were the platitudes about toeing the line, respecting superiors and not bucking the system. What replaced it was Norm, not Ahmed; the past, not the future.

Alex Buzo, of course, didn't have an agenda, apart from being a good writer, and if he had lived in one of the imperialist states, even a fading one, like Britain, that might have been enough, and he might have achieved the fame a Tom Stoppard, for example, did; but Buzo lived in a subaltern state whose primary purpose was to serve, and to provide soldiers for the imperial wars and the occasional entertainer, like Rolf Harris, to amuse. And so in his case, geography was destiny. We can't blame him for not solving racism. Racism at the time was barely understood and even the term itself was controversial. But looking back now from the vantage point of forty-five years, it seems profoundly sad that his play has hardly aged, and the vile opinions so fulsomely expressed sound so completely contemporary in an Australia where Aboriginal children are still malnourished and refugees from the wars we happily endorse are routinely locked up by the Government because they tried to 'jump the queue'.

What would have happened if Buzo had tried to dig beneath the colourful language into the places where that language was forged, if he had shown us not only *what* we were like, but *why* we were like it? What would Australia be like now if that moment of standing up and stretching our collective imagination had not been squandered under the illusion it would last forever, and the small changes that it was able to force through were not so quickly reversed. Because there was a revolution after all, a revolution in the traditional sense of a return to the former position. Australia was returned to its former position, supine at the feet of a foreign power, and in theatre the experiment of Graeme Blundell and his colleagues to challenge bourgeois theatre was over. There was still theatre, of course, and even more of it; and Australian, too. And very funny. And bourgeois was the new norm.

This essay first appeared as part of the Cue the Chorus series, published by Currency Press and funded by the CAL Cultural Fund.

References:

1. Led by the Three Bards, Adam Mickiewicz, Juliusz Słowacki and Zygmunt Krasiński. Chopin, of course was a great Polish nationalist as well. See, Porter B. *When Nationalism Began to Hate: Imagining Modern Politics in Nineteenth-Century Poland,* Oxford University Press

2. 21 year old Errol Noack

3. Graeme Blundell, *Talking Heads with Peter Thompson*, ABC Radio, 29/06/2009

4. Noted because Norm soon proves to be something else as well, an inveterate liar.

5. The Wobblies is a nickname for the Industrial Workers of the World, a radical international union formed in 1905.

6. The Vietnamese, tellingly, refer to the conflict as "The American War".

7. "Kill Whitlam" Murdoch ordered his editors, according to a secret diplomatic telegram dated January 20, 1975 released by the US National Archives and reported in the Sydney Morning Herald, June 28, 2014.

8. As the building housing the resident Australian Performing Group was called.

9. The ALP'S winning slogan in the 1972 election, in which the arts played a prominent role.

10. It's worth remembering that 1971 was the first year Aboriginal people were counted in the Australian census as *people*.

11. And sent them reeling.

12. John Romeril was one of the few avowedly political playwrights of the time, meaning that he took a position *critical* of entrenched power. Dorothy Hewett, from a slightly earlier period, was proudly communist.

13. Bob Ellis Obituary, *Sydney Morning Herald*, 18/8/06

14. In fact, his discovery of the play.

15. 1968, Old Tote

16. Edwin Hodgeman

17. Though Jacques Lacan *did* famously retort to the student revolutionaries of 1968 "As hysterics, you demand a new master. You will get it!"

18. Sylvia Plath, *Daddy,* Ariel, 1963

19. Bob Hawke, June 13, 1983 "Remarks of the President and Prime Minister Robert Hawke of Australia Following Their Meetings ," June 13, 1983. Online by Gerhard Peters and John T. Woolley, *The American Presidency*

ALSO AVAILABLE FROM CURRENCY PRESS:

Shafana and Aunt Sarrinah
Alana Valentine

What do you do when you disagree with someone you love? Wearing a hijab is a touchstone of religious identity, but it is also imbued with a complex array of historical and contemporary meanings. In Alana Valentine's new play, the cultural meaning of the hijab has become a wedge between generations. At the heart of *Shafana and Aunt Sarrinah* is the relationship between an aunt and her niece. Both devout Muslims, the younger woman wants to put on a headscarf, the older woman tries to dissuade her. For Aunt Sarrinah, the hijab represents a world from which she has escaped; for her niece, Shafana, it is a personal statement of renewed faith.

ISBN 978-0-86819-882-8

Cue the Chorus essays

Seventeen contemporary responses to seventeen classic Australian plays, *Cue the Chorus* is an essay series from Currency Press in association with the Copyright Agency Limited. The series is written by respected Australian playwrights offering insights into the work of their peers.

Featuring contributions from: Jada Alberts, Van Badham, Hilary Bell, Angela Betzien, Wesley Enoch, John Harding, Tom Holloway, Finegan Kruckemeyer, Linda Jaivin, Andrea James, Noëlle Janaczewska, Kate Mulvany, Roslyn Oades, Hannie Rayson, Melissa Reeves, Stephen Sewell and Alana Valentine.

The Stephen Sewell essay in this book is from *Cue the Chorus*. Read others in the series for free at http://www.currency.com.au/cuethechorus.aspx.

Tales from the Arabian Nights
Donna Abela

In this delightful adaptation of the classic tales, Donna Abela brings centuries-old tradition into the modern era with a play that is timeless yet utterly contemporary. The play centres on a king who punishes refugees (aka 'smuggles') who flee to his land; but a series of stories told to him by one imprisoned smuggle eventually thaws his heart. Abela has created an imaginative and playful piece of theatre for young people that begs many questions and longer discussions about the treatment of displaced and desperate people.

ISBN 978-176-0622-756

Single Asian Female
Michelle Law

The Golden Phoenix, a restaurant on the Sunshine Coast. The last customers have left for the night, and Pearl can unwind. She's the quintessential matriarch–balancing family, business, and her love of karaoke. Enter her daughters: Zoe, in the throes of online dating, making big life decisions. And Mei, a teenager, grappling with her identity in modern Australia. Of course they see the world differently to their mother. Pearl is the classic (hilarious) onslaught of embarrassing observations, constantly questioning her Westernised children. Tonight she reveals a secret that threatens to tear their family apart.

ISBN 978-176-0621-810

www.currency.com.au

Visit Currency Press' website now to:

- Buy your books online
- Browse through our full list of titles, from plays to screenplays, books on theatre, film and music, and more
- Choose a play for your school or amateur performance group by cast size and gender
- Obtain information about performance rights
- Find out about theatre productions and other performing arts news across Australia
- For students, read our study guides
- For teachers, access syllabus and other relevant information
- Sign up for our email newsletter

www.ingramcontent.com/pod-product-compliance
Lightning Source LLC
Chambersburg PA
CBHW050028090426
42734CB00021B/3461